My First Time

Getting a Dog

by Jeri Cipriano

LOOK! BOOKS™

Red Chair Press Egremont, Massachusetts

Look! Books are produced and published by Red Chair Press:
Red Chair Press LLC PO Box 333 South Egremont, MA 01258-0333

FREE Educator Guides at www.redchairpress.com/free-resources

The publisher thanks the Central Oklahoma Humane Society
for its help in preparing this book and its resources.

Publisher's Cataloging-In-Publication Data

Names: Cipriano, Jeri, author.

Title: Getting a dog / by Jeri Cipriano.

Description: Egremont, Massachusetts : Red Chair Press, [2021] | Series: Look! books. My first time | Includes index and a list of resources for further reading. | Interest age level: 005-008. | Summary: "Getting a new pet can be an exciting and fun experience. But getting a dog comes with a lot of responsibility. To be sure you are ready for the big job ahead, learn about things you will need to do to make your dog happy in its new home"--Provided by publisher.

Identifiers: ISBN 9781643710921 (RLB hardcover) | ISBN 9781643710983 (softcover) | ISBN 9781643711041 (ebook)

Subjects: LCSH: Dogs--Juvenile literature. | Dog adoption--Juvenile literature. | CYAC: Dogs. | Dog adoption.

Classification: LCC SF426.5 .C56 2021 (print) | LCC SF426.5 (ebook) | DDC 636.7/0887--dc23

LCCN: 2020948759

Copyright © 2022 Red Chair Press LLC
RED CHAIR PRESS, the RED CHAIR and associated logos are registered trademarks of Red Chair Press LLC.

All rights reserved. No part of this book may be reproduced, stored in an information or retrieval system, or transmitted in any form by any means, electronic, mechanical including photocopying, recording, or otherwise without the prior written permission from the Publisher. For permissions, contact info@redchairpress.com

Photo credits: iStock

Printed in United States of America
0421 1P CGF21

Table of Contents

All About Dogs

Are you thinking of getting a pet? A dog is a good choice as a pet. Just remember: Dogs always need a person to take care of them their whole life.

All puppies are cute. But puppies grow into adult dogs. So, you have to decide what type of dog you want.

Do you want a big dog or a small dog?

Do you want a dog that needs lots of exercise? Or a dog that enjoys lying around?

Pick a Puppy

Some people know what **breed** or kind of dog they want. They choose the puppy they want about one month after it is born.

They come back for the puppy when it is ready to leave its mother—at eight to ten weeks old or more.

Good to Know

Here's how to hold a puppy: Put one hand under it. Put the other hand gently around its body.

How Puppies Grow

Most puppies are born with sisters and brothers. The whole group of puppies is called a **litter**.

Good to Know

Two puppies from the same litter are called "litter mates." They are "play mates," too!

Birth
A puppy's eyes are closed when it is born. It cannot yet hear.

Two to Three Weeks

At two weeks, a puppy can see. Its eyes are blue. Over time, the color darkens.

At three weeks, a puppy can hear.

Meal Time

For four weeks, puppies drink only their mother's milk for food.

Mother's Love

The mother licks the puppies to clean them. The puppy feels safe when she does that.

Four Weeks

At four weeks, the puppy has little teeth. Now it can eat solid food.

Getting Ready

Dogs that look alike may belong to the same breed. But many dogs are mixed breeds. No two mixes look the same.

Good to Know

You can get your new pet from a dog breeder or an animal shelter. Animal shelters have puppies and older dogs. Get to know a few dogs before you make up your mind.

What You Will Need

A puppy collar
Attach a dog tag that has your dog's name and your family name and phone number.

A crate
Your puppy will stay safe in its crate when no one is home. Remember: Never leave a puppy alone for more than 3 or 4 hours.

Meal Time
Buy two bowls—one for water and one for food. Get a "scoop" you will use for your dog's food.

Cleaning Up
Have the right cleaning items ready in case of "accidents."

Toys
Puppies like to chew things. You might want to buy a few different toys.

Choosing Your Pet

Spend time with your puppy's mother. Is she the kind of dog you want your puppy to be when it is grown? Is she friendly?

Watch how the puppies behave. Sit with them. Which puppy is shy? Which is friendly? Which is happy and wags its tail?

Choose the puppy you want. A healthy puppy smells a little like milk. It has a cool, wet nose.

You can take your puppy home when it is eight- or ten-weeks old. Hold the puppy on your lap for the ride home. Bring a soft blanket. It calms the puppy. Plus, you have it in case the puppy pees or gets sick.

Welcome Home

You will want to see a **veterinarian**, or animal doctor, after you bring your puppy home. The vet will make sure that your new pet is healthy.

Chow Time!

Show your new pet where it will find its meals. Always leave a bowl of fresh water out. Make sure to wash and dry your dog's bowls each day.

Buy food made for puppies. Ask your vet for **brands** of food that are good for your dog.

Give your puppy small meals three or four times a day. When your pet is older it will need only one or two meals each day.

Treats

Give your dog a treat when it is good or when it does what you ask it to do.

Goodnight

Your puppy will sleep in its crate. Cover three sides of the crate so your puppy can feel safe and cozy. Keep the crate in your room so your new pet will not be afraid.

Ah Choo!

Some people sneeze around dust or fur. These people often can't own dogs. Most dogs shed, or drop, fur around the house.

The only kind of dog that does not shed fur is a dog with hair for its **coat**. A poodle is a type of dog that has hair, not fur.

One Doodle, Two Doodles, Three Doodles, Four!

Poodles and mixed breeds of poodles with different types of dogs are hair dogs, too.

Poodle

Labrador Retriever

Labradoodle

Poodle

Golden Retriever

Golden Doodle

Poodle

Cocker Spaniel

Cockerpoo

What Is Your Pet Saying?

Your dog doesn't speak. But you can tell what is on its mind. Dogs use their bodies to "talk." If you watch carefully, you'll know what your dog is trying to tell you.

This dog is a happy dog. See its smile?

Begging

If your dog touches you with its paw, it wants something. It may want to be petted. It may want to go out. It may simply want food.

Begging

The Play-Bow

Your dog wants to play when it **crouches** on its front legs with its bottom in the air. Sometimes it wags its tail, too.

Paws Up

Paws Up

Is your dog laying on its back with its paws in the air? Your dog is saying that you are the boss and it wants a belly rub.

Happy Dog!

Your dog is usually very happy to see you. It will wag its tail. Its face will show love and a doggie "smile."

Barks

Your dog may bark to tell you someone is at the door. Some dogs howl when they are lonely. Some whine when they want attention.

Stepping Out

Your puppy will need to go out after each time it eats. Take the puppy to the same spot. This will teach it what to do. A puppy needs to go out every 3 or 4 hours. This is called "puppy training."

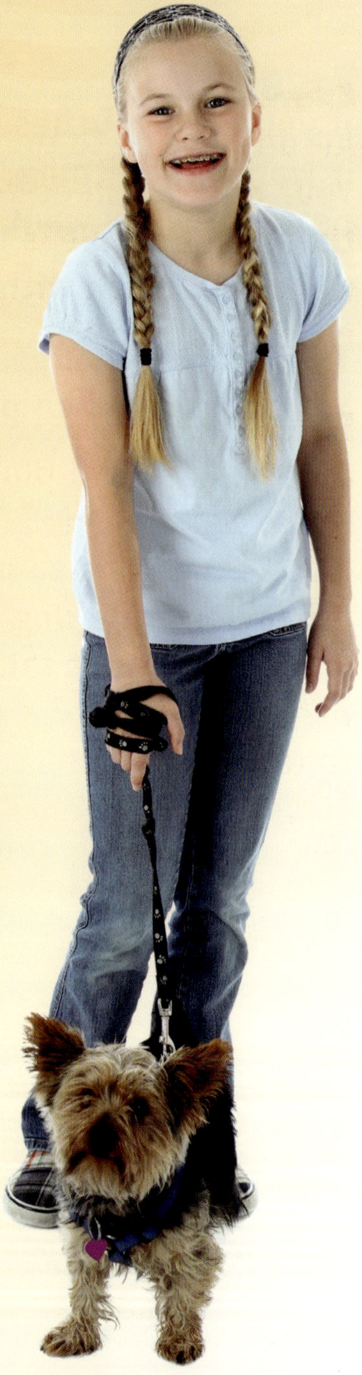

When taking your dog to pee or poop use words like "Go potty" to train him to respond.

Exercise

All dogs need to go out for exercise. Your dog will need to be walked 3 to 4 times a day. This is when it learns to walk on a leash without pulling. This is "school" time.

Play Time

All dogs need to play outside. Some chase balls. Some play with flying discs. Some like to play with other dogs in a dog park.

You must not take your dog *off* its leash until it is trained and follows important commands.

- COME
- SIT and SIT STAY
- DOWN and DOWN STAY

Time for Training

Take your puppy outside—about every two hours—and immediately after he wakes up from a nap, after playing, and after eating or drinking.

Praise your puppy every time he pees outdoors—you can even give him a treat—but remember to do so as soon after he's finished peeing or pooping, so he knows it was the right thing to do.

Words to Know

brand: the name of a company that sells something

breed: a group of animals that look alike

coat: an animal's covering of fur or hair

crouches: when the upper body is brought forward and down

litter: all the animals that are born from the same mother at the same time

veterinarian: a doctor trained to treat animals

Learn More at the Library

Check out these books to learn more.

Arlon, Penelope and Gordon-Harris, Tory. *Puppies and Kittens.* Scholastic, 2013.

Wheeler-Toppen, Jodi. *Dog Science Unleashed.* National Geographic Kids, 2018.

Zachary, Paul. *Caring for My New Puppy.* Mitchell Lane, 2018.

Index

About the Author

Jeri Cipriano enjoys writing for children of all ages. She loves to learn new things she can share with others.